D1301740

Denise Marsh was born and raised in Brooklyn, New York. She still has the accent and can tell you where to get the cheapest and best pizza!

Denise's mom instilled in her a love for reading and a passion for writing at a young age. She learned that trips to the library were an adventure and how important the spoken word is.

Denise has been an Elementary school teacher for the last 19 years. She taught in Brooklyn, NY and continues to teach in Palm Beach County. She has always had a love for children and building their self-esteem. Denise hosts a poetry club at her school twice a year for lower and upper grades. One of her greatest challenges is trying to multitask but she continues to persevere. Denise resides in West Palm Beach, Florida with her very precocious and funny 12-year-old son. She enjoys writing, reading, journaling, swimming, Karaoke with friends, going to the movies and doing poetry readings.

Bill,

Thank you for your beautiful music + friendship. I'm very proud of your accomplishments + happy to have you in my life

love,

Denise Marsh

Fight Song

Like a small boat
On the ocean
Sending big waves
Into motion
Like how a single word
Can make a heart open
I might only have one match
But I can make an explosion

And all those things I didn't say
Wrecking balls inside my brain
I will scream them loud tonight
Can you hear my voice this time?

This is my fight song
Take back my life song
Prove I'm alright song
My power's turned on
Starting right now I'll be strong
I'll play my fight song
And I don't really care if nobody else believes
'Cause I've still got a lot of fight left in me

Losing friends and I'm chasing sleep
Everybody's worried about me
In too deep
Say I'm in too deep (in too deep)
And it's been two years I miss my home
But there's a fire burning in my bones
Still believe
Yeah, I still believe

And all those things I didn't say
Wrecking balls inside my brain
I will scream them loud tonight
Can you hear my voice this time?

This is my fight song
Take back my life song
Prove I'm alright song
My power's turned on
Starting right now I'll be strong
I'll play my fight song
And I don't really care if nobody else believes
'Cause I've still got a lot of fight left in me
A lot of fight left in me

Like a small boat
On the ocean
Sending big waves
Into motion
Like how a single word
Can make a heart open
I might only have one match
But I can make an explosion

This is my fight song
Take back my life song
Prove I'm alright song
My power's turned on
Starting right now I'll be strong (I'll be strong)
I'll play my fight song
And I don't really care if nobody else believes
'Cause I've still got a lot of fight left in me
Know I've still got a lot of fight left in me

Songwriters: Dave Bassett / Rachel Platten

My so-called "relationship" with cancer

QUIET is the FIRE SILENT is the FLAME

First Edition

Wellington, Florida, USA

2019

Dedication

I am sure that if I were to honor and acknowledge everyone that has been a part of this journey there would not be enough pages.

I would like to thank my twin sister, Marilyn who always made me feel brave from the beginning to the end.

For Christine G for washing my hair, dropping off food in my fridge at all hours in the night and personally installing a hose shower tool so I could take a normal shower without getting bandages wet .

Thank you to Sue who went with me to nearly every single doctor appointment, holding my hand, giving nurturing, understanding and tough love (especially when I talked about pulling a "Thelma and Louise" escape instead of going to a very serious appointment.) Thank you to the Reyes family for their prayer circle and enlightening daily messages.

Thank you to Jane and Jean for their prayers and lifting me despite the miles. ..my "heart sisters ".

Then there are the people who helped with the "before" and "after". I would like to acknowledge Lisa and Julie for rallying support amongst my colleagues at my Elementary school Discovery key- because the love and support I got was nothing short of amazing.

Thank you to Tina for driving my son back and forth to school when I couldn't drive. Thank you to my understanding principal Catherine Lewis who let me leave school every day to have radiation treatments and who understood how leaving the kids in my classroom was one of the most heart wrenching days of my life.

Thank you to Christie for making me laugh in the hospital when I wanted to cry and not leaving my side even when the ugliest personality would surface in those days of darkness.

A warm thank you is also extended to Teresa who never stopped checking up on me and made me claim my sanity with humor and positivity. So many to name. Thank you to Kelly for your essential oils that comforted me and for letting the tears flow and flow. Thank you for my Discovery Key Family of teachers, staff, and parents who pushed and supported me - Literally. Thank you to Janine for rallying support and helping with all the disability paperwork. I could not have made it financially without the help of Debra F who was able to share my story and secure financial assistance through ThinkPink for Kids! Then there was my little tokens of love. The phone calls...My friend Nancy holding my hand, taking me to lunch and folding my laundry.

The fruit arrangement from my dear friend Danielle A. My wonderful breast surgeon, Dr. Kleban, for being tough with me but nurturing. Also, Dr. Eidelman and his caring staff at Plastic Surgery of the Palm Beaches for explaining every step of my reconstruction process and molding me into an image that still has made me feel beautiful....

Then there was the "after". A huge thank you and hug to Stephanie, a caring radiation technician at SFRO who literally gave me life and who had probably never seen so many tears and wondered how I could still tell jokes! I couldn't have processed all the 'madness' without my outstanding Oncologist Marilyn Raymond at Florida Cancer Specialists.

Thank you to my landlord Phil for being so patient when rent was VERY late. Thank you to the love of my life, my son Daniel who gave me so many reasons to keep fighting.

Thank you to Kelly T for sharing her journey and encouraging me every step of the way.

Thank you to my mother in heaven who died of Breast Cancer for providing spiritual guidance through dreams, symbols and signs.

Thank you to Desi whose tough journey with cancer taught me how strength, love and humor will see you through.

Again, if I forgot you. You really are not forgotten. You are all and will continue to be an integral part of my journey.

Thank you to my amazing first grade team — to Fara who kindly grabbed me with the first, "I'm so sorry embrace" when I told her about the shocking first diagnosis (over the phone), letting me put my head down and cry my eyes out as she summoned administration. To sweet Erin, Trisha and Gabby who came to visit me, feed my hamster, and made me laugh. Finally, to thoughtful Jamie who lent me her collection of romantic comedies.

QUIET is the FIRE - SILENT is the FLAME:
My so-called "relationship" with cancer

The Diagnosis:

The Beginning of the End

Pause you who read this, and think for a moment of the long chain of iron or gold, of thorns or flowers, that would never have bound you, but for the formation of the first link on one memorable day.

Charles Dickens, Great Expectations

Ode to my Breasts

My apologies
Condolences....
Tears
and hugs.
So sorry....
Burial of a part
of my person.
No one understands...
Four hours of
Surgery.
Masks.
Anesthesia.
Scrubs
Vomiting.
Sharpies.
Scalpels.
Blood runs
Through drains
Everyday
Showing me
Your **Death....**
I'm sorry....

D.o.d. 5/6/16

Burning Question

After surgery...
After pathology...
After the last line...
Afterthought...
After Signature ...
And stamps...
After documentation
Print and type...
Where do the parts go???

WHERE DO MY PARTS GO???

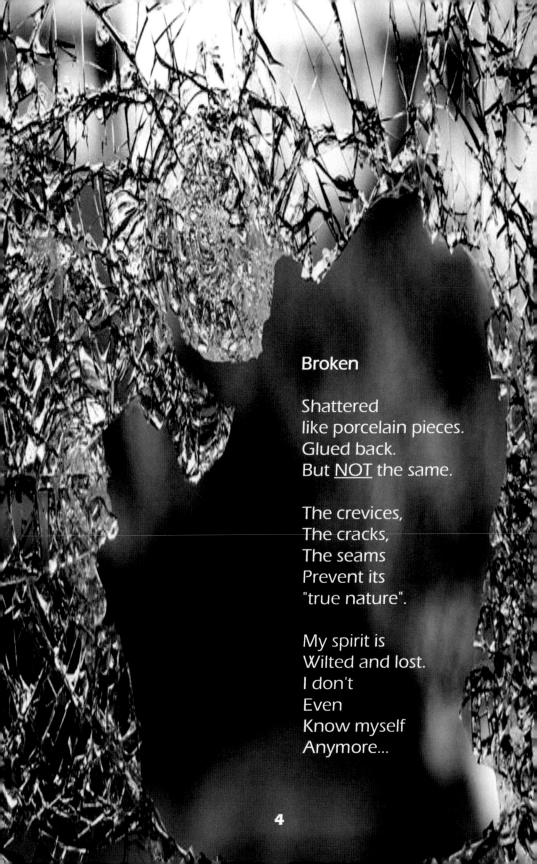

Broken

Shattered
like porcelain pieces.
Glued back.
But <u>NOT</u> the same.

The crevices,
The cracks,
The seams
Prevent its
"true nature".

My spirit is
Wilted and lost.
I don't
Even
Know myself
Anymore...

4

Riddle Cruel

Spirit crushed
Fantasies flushed
Dreams scattered
Cancer flattered
Rhythm and rhyme.
How does a soul break
Into pieces?
Ask Cancer....

Pathology Report

Numbers
Signs
Stages-
All the same.
"This is your cancer".
"This is the next step".
My head spinning...
Diagnosis daydream -
I wish....
Not
Your mama's
Report card.

Flood

Tears flooding
My brain
Insufficient
Intolerable
Insolvent
I am
D
R
O
W
N
I
G
In tears....

Cancer Chain

What do you want?

Knocking down my door

Barging into my life

Hunting me down....

Your chain of poison

Will **NOT**

Survive
My
Spirit...

Lost

No directions

Compass missing
in the distance.
No one in sight....

Lost
Beyond
Belief.

STOP!

Stop telling me

"it's okay"

"You are so strong"

"I can't even imagine..."

"You'll just get a cool wig"

" I have a friend who had cancer.."

STOP talking

And telling!

STOP asking questions!

Can't you see?

I don't know anything...

I just

DON'T want

To KNOW anymore

Because all I do is

Know ... Know... Know

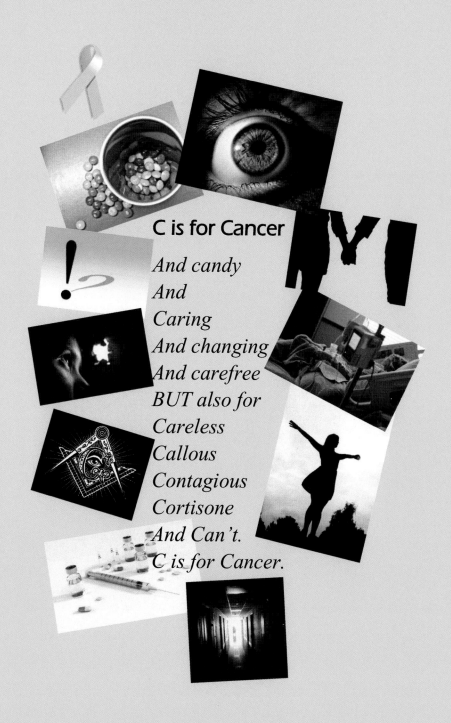

C is for Cancer

And candy
And
Caring
And changing
And carefree
BUT also for
Careless
Callous
Contagious
Cortisone
And Can't.
C is for Cancer.

Friendship and Support

If you can't fly, then run.
If you can't run, then walk.
If you can't walk, then crawl.
But whatever you do, you have to keep
moving forward

Martin Luther King Jr.

Angel in Pink

Survivor.

Warrior.

Angel in pink.
You appeared
in a foamy mist.
A labyrinth
of weak spirit
and physical pain.

Healer.
Calmer.
Solace bringer.
Heart Keeper.
Graceful for you
For always.

For Christine

At My Door

By my window,
At my door,
Like sunshine
You show up
Full of life
And light
And lift me.
I love you...
My beautiful friend–
Who is
Always,
Thankfully
At my door...

For Stephanie my nurturing Radiology Technician who literally gave me life.

Treatment 4... thirty-six more to go.

Please radiation. Please work!

Waves

Red light

Green light...

Wrapped like

a package

with too much tape.

Robotic wave

Circumference

Perfectly calcu...

My life

In your waves.

Ironic....

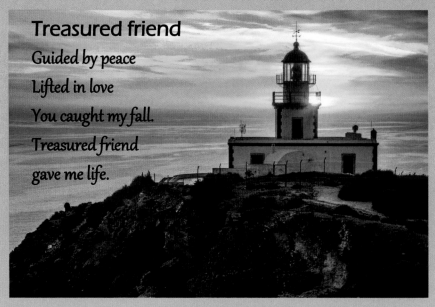

Treasured friend
Guided by peace
Lifted in love
You caught my fall.
Treasured friend
gave me life.

My journey
rests on
jagged rocks.
Treasured friend
never let go.

Your voice
Your heart
My shield.
Grateful
I am.

For Christy B. the Nurturer

Support

Scattered tears
You pull me up.
DISCOURAGED
DISCOUNTED
you share my tears
You
Cook
And plan.
You
Talk

And walk
And pray-

Friend,
You have me
in your beautiful heart
and my scattered tears
now have a home.

Love, Longing, and Relationships

Being deeply loved by someone gives you strength while loving someone deeply gives you courage

Lao Tzu

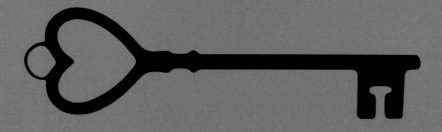

For the love of my life: my son, Daniel

Choking

Choking with sadness
My beautiful boy.
I love you–
My heart
My soul...
I live for you
I work for you.
Your life
MUST be good...
Choking...so you know–
You are
My world.

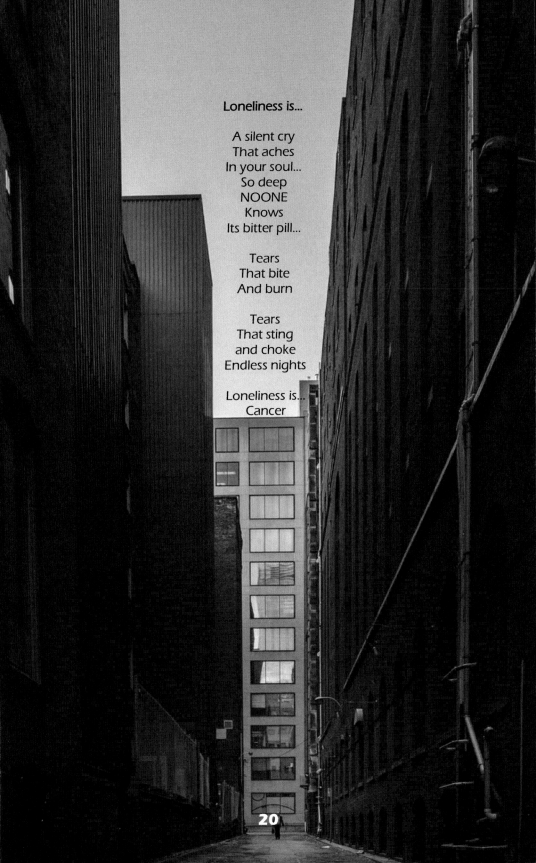

Loneliness is...

A silent cry
That aches
In your soul...
So deep
NOONE
Knows
Its bitter pill...

Tears
That bite
And burn

Tears
That sting
and choke
Endless nights

Loneliness is...
Cancer

Drought

Cruelest libido
Mock my shame
Only cancer is to blame.
Desire burning
Pages turning.
Diagnosis all showing:
DEATH OF LIBIDO
Cruel fate
Too much to contemplate.

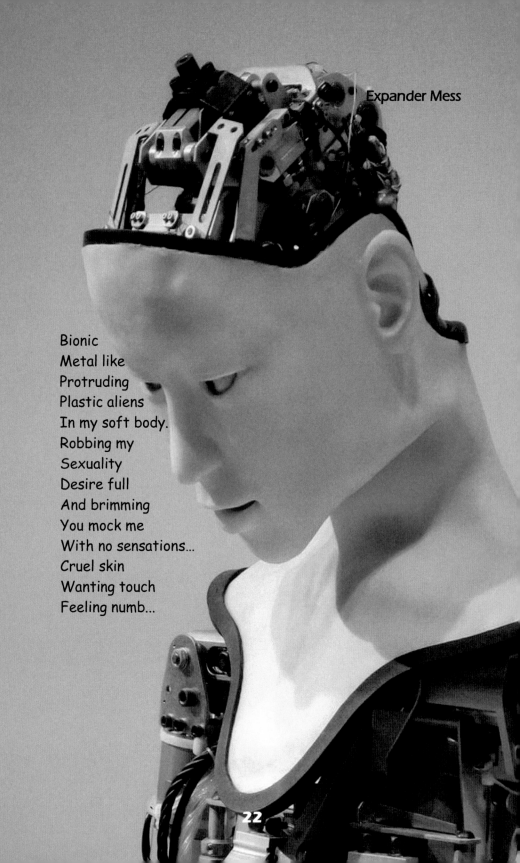

Expander Mess

Bionic
Metal like
Protruding
Plastic aliens
In my soft body.
Robbing my
Sexuality
Desire full
And brimming
You mock me
With no sensations...
Cruel skin
Wanting touch
Feeling numb...

22

Famine

My touch
My love
My space
My passion...
Beyond
Control
And level
I quiver
With the slightest touch.
STARVING....

Wanting my "real" body back...

For Mike:

Also a Cancer Survivor

Angel

You whispered
In the cold darkness
and filled my world
With light and fragrance.
Online strangers we are-
Distant
We are NOT-
You
Touch
My soul.

Warning

Desire floods
It knows no limits.
Cross to bear
Cancer Care
Flood in...
Flood out...
Bathing the shore,
Carrying the tide.
Inhaling
Exhaling...

Will you still swim with me
when the sharks
are in the water?

Fighting the fight. Terrified of treatment options. How can I hold on to vanity?

Army

Battling soldiers.
Stakes are high,
Protecting the fortress.
Ammunition low
Treacherous fight.
How can we cut the losses
Again
And again?
Is retreat
Inevitable???

Soaring

The sail
once tattered
And burned
Unable to sail
Just holding
A strong
Sad
Vigil
Now flies high
proud
And fierce
Sailing happily
In the wind.

Types of Rain

In the rain
Against the slippery window pane
Watching the tears
March and roll up and down
In a continuous path
The rain stopped
and with the
storm's aftermath
my tears
continue to roll
When would they stop?
I wondered
Wonder
AM
wondering
WHEN?

Fragile

Eyes of blue steel
　　　Icy oceans
　　　I want to swim in.
　　　Fragile you
Fragile me...

I see your rope
　　　Its frayed
　　　But strong
　　　Reaching out-
　　　Pulling you in.
　　　Feel the safety
It is
All around you.

Zero

Hopelessness is
NOT a disease.
It is NOT an excuse
Or a facade-
It exists.

Struggle of course
Can make you brave
BUT
It can also
Bleed you
Rob you
And tear away
The wall of strength
You ascertained
In one
Split
Second.

Jaded Jigsaw

Making the pieces fit
even the odd ones
That have to be bent
Or shoved in.

Looked so easy at first glance
Then the time
The effort
The care
Till every piece fits compatibly.

What about the pieces that are
Frayed
Mangled
Discarded-
Where will they go
when they fit
No one's puzzle?

The After: Reflections

"Courage is not the absence of fear,
But rather the judgment that something
Else is more important than fear."

Ambrose Redmoon

Sobbing to Mike

Time Warped

Tick Tock
Goes the clock
Cars in ignition
Sunrises
Doors slamming
School buses en route
Breakfast cooking
Coffee steaming...
Even the squirrel
Is busy searching
For daily whims
As I lay here
Frozen...
Tick Tock

quiet fire

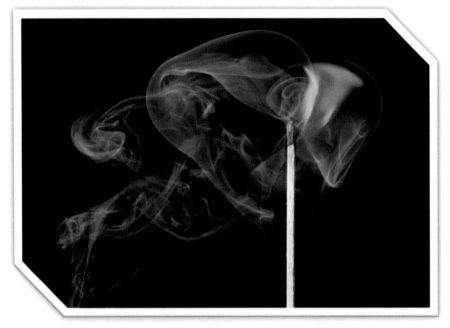

I will not be quiet

nor docile.
I will not be accepting
and just be grateful.
I will not make excuses
or exceptions
for my dreams
are setting
a quiet fire.

I will feed this fire
Because it is FREEDOM
And it is MINE.

It is never over...it's all about stages...

Infinite

Surgery is not over
when it's over.
Clip, pull, tuck.
Bleed. Bleed. Bleed.
They think it's about speed...

Wounds and bandages
can't protect nor can they hide
a body here
for an endless ride.

Healing creams,
salves and blends -
all here until the bitter end.

A torn heart.
A few calm screams.
Coming apart at the seams.

A savage mind,
that revisits the pain
till you feel insane.

Surgery is one part -
The mind and body -
so tough to restart.

Suddenly a partnership
no longer -
Each on its own
A new body is sewn.

Everyone has an opinion.... It is okay to feel different.

It wasn't YOUR Cancer
It was all MINE-
The pain
The turmoil
The diagnosis
The treatment
It is...
It was...
ALL MINE.

Don't criticize
My reasons
My decisions.

Don't negate
My purpos
My life...
Because
your choices
Are different.

It is...
It was...

MY Cancer

Just yesterday

Three years ago
seasons did their timely dance.

Three years ago
I sat in this
SAME
Surgery room-
Sharpies
with angry arrows
marked for my
MASSACRE-
Breasts up for
SLAUGHTER...
Cancer,
You PREDATOR...
Anger still not unleashed

Three years ago
A story in pastels-
Angled photos
to timeline
Each moment
Of SABOTAGE.

Three years ago
and now I see
a computer file
devoid of heart
highlighting each graphic detail
chiseled to abbreviations and encryption.

Three years ago I thought my pain was over
yet my soul weeps for yesterday.

Sign of the Times

Gathered in a room
like wilted flowers.
White-haired folks,
canes and walkers
and there I stood-
No white hair
No cane to highlight my
age.
Our leader, cancer
has brought us together.
Some fresh to the "club"
others in treatment
and some like me-
In remission.
Cancer
CHOSE us.
It is our bridge.

Vision

If you turn around
and you pick up speed,
Sometimes the grass,
the flowers and
even the birds
in the sky
meet your glance.
And their stare
In all its wonder,
beckons for you.

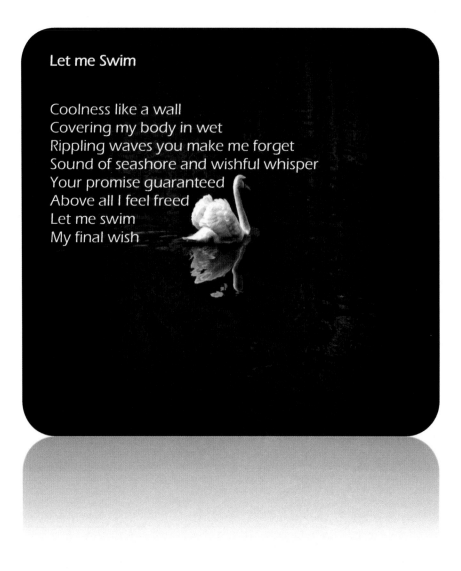

Let me Swim

Coolness like a wall
Covering my body in wet
Rippling waves you make me forget
Sound of seashore and wishful whisper
Your promise guaranteed
Above all I feel freed
Let me swim
My final wish

Made in the USA
Columbia, SC
12 November 2019

83111251R00029